50 Cooking with Coconut Milk Recipes

By: Kelly Johnson

Table of Contents

- Coconut Milk Chicken Curry
- Vegan Coconut Milk Rice Pudding
- Thai Coconut Milk Soup (Tom Kha)
- Coconut Milk and Mango Smoothie
- Coconut Milk Shrimp Scampi
- Coconut Milk Pancakes
- Creamy Coconut Milk Mashed Potatoes
- Coconut Milk Chia Pudding
- Coconut Milk Tofu Stir-Fry
- Coconut Curry Lentils
- Coconut Milk Ice Cream
- Coconut Milk Chicken Soup
- Vegan Coconut Milk Chocolate Mousse
- Coconut Milk Smoothie Bowl
- Coconut Milk Rice Pilaf
- Spicy Coconut Milk Noodles
- Coconut Milk Braised Beef
- Coconut Milk Tapioca Pudding
- Coconut Milk Mango Lassi
- Coconut and Lime Shrimp
- Coconut Milk Panna Cotta
- Coconut Milk and Almond Cake
- Coconut Milk Quinoa Salad
- Coconut Milk Popsicles
- Coconut Milk Rice with Turmeric
- Coconut Milk Roasted Squash Soup
- Coconut Milk & Chia Breakfast Porridge
- Coconut Milk Vegan Mac and Cheese
- Coconut Milk and Lemon Curd Tart
- Spicy Coconut Milk Fish Curry
- Coconut Milk and Banana Smoothie
- Coconut Milk Porridge with Fruit
- Coconut Milk Chicken and Sweet Potato Stew
- Coconut Milk Gravy for Biscuits
- Coconut Milk and Pineapple Chutney

- Coconut Milk Cauliflower Soup
- Coconut Milk Scones with Jam
- Coconut Milk Vegetable Stew
- Thai Coconut Milk Curry
- Coconut Milk Brown Rice Pudding
- Coconut Milk Green Smoothie
- Coconut Milk Ice Cream Bars
- Coconut Milk Caramel Sauce
- Coconut Milk Granola Bars
- Coconut Milk Banana Bread
- Coconut Milk Pumpkin Soup
- Coconut Milk Rice Cake
- Coconut Milk Spiced Pudding
- Coconut Milk Smoothie with Berries
- Coconut Milk Chicken Tikka Masala

Coconut Milk Chicken Curry

Ingredients:

- 1 lb chicken breast, cubed
- 1 can (14 oz) coconut milk
- 1 onion, diced
- 2 garlic cloves, minced
- 1 tbsp grated ginger
- 2 tbsp curry powder
- 1 tsp ground turmeric
- 1/2 tsp ground cumin
- 1/2 tsp paprika
- Salt and pepper to taste
- 1 tbsp olive oil
- 1/2 cup chicken broth
- 1 tbsp cilantro, chopped (optional)

Instructions:

1. Heat olive oil in a large pan over medium heat. Add the diced onion and sauté for 3-4 minutes until softened.
2. Add garlic and ginger and sauté for another minute.
3. Stir in the curry powder, turmeric, cumin, and paprika, cooking for 1-2 minutes to release the flavors.
4. Add the chicken cubes and cook until browned on all sides.
5. Pour in the coconut milk and chicken broth. Bring to a simmer, then reduce heat and let it cook for 20 minutes or until the chicken is cooked through and the sauce has thickened.
6. Season with salt and pepper to taste. Garnish with chopped cilantro before serving.

Vegan Coconut Milk Rice Pudding

Ingredients:

- 1 can (14 oz) coconut milk
- 1 cup Arborio rice
- 2 cups water
- 1/4 cup sugar
- 1 tsp vanilla extract
- 1/2 tsp cinnamon
- Pinch of salt

Instructions:

1. In a saucepan, combine coconut milk, water, and rice. Bring to a boil over medium heat, then reduce to a simmer.
2. Stir occasionally and cook for about 20-25 minutes, or until the rice is tender and the liquid has thickened.
3. Add sugar, vanilla extract, cinnamon, and a pinch of salt. Stir well and cook for another 5 minutes.
4. Remove from heat and let it sit for a few minutes before serving. Serve warm or chilled.

Thai Coconut Milk Soup (Tom Kha)

Ingredients:

- 1 can (14 oz) coconut milk
- 2 cups vegetable broth
- 2 stalks lemongrass, bruised
- 3-4 kaffir lime leaves, torn
- 1 inch ginger, sliced
- 1 cup sliced mushrooms
- 1 medium tomato, quartered
- 1/2 cup tofu, cubed (or chicken)
- 1 tbsp soy sauce
- 1 tbsp lime juice
- 1 tsp chili paste or fresh chilies (optional)
- Fresh cilantro for garnish

Instructions:

1. In a large pot, combine the coconut milk, vegetable broth, lemongrass, lime leaves, and ginger. Bring to a boil.
2. Add mushrooms, tomato, and tofu. Simmer for 15-20 minutes until the flavors meld and the vegetables soften.
3. Stir in soy sauce, lime juice, and chili paste. Taste and adjust seasoning with additional soy sauce or lime juice if needed.
4. Remove lemongrass stalks and lime leaves. Garnish with fresh cilantro and serve hot.

Coconut Milk and Mango Smoothie

Ingredients:

- 1 ripe mango, peeled and chopped
- 1 cup coconut milk
- 1/2 cup ice cubes
- 1 tbsp honey or agave (optional)
- 1/2 tsp vanilla extract (optional)

Instructions:

1. In a blender, combine mango, coconut milk, ice, honey, and vanilla extract.
2. Blend until smooth. If the smoothie is too thick, add more coconut milk to reach your desired consistency.
3. Pour into glasses and serve chilled.

Coconut Milk Shrimp Scampi

Ingredients:

- 1 lb shrimp, peeled and deveined
- 1 can (14 oz) coconut milk
- 3 cloves garlic, minced
- 1 tbsp olive oil
- 1 tbsp butter
- Juice of 1 lemon
- Salt and pepper to taste
- 1/2 tsp red pepper flakes (optional)
- Fresh parsley, chopped for garnish

Instructions:

1. In a large pan, heat olive oil and butter over medium heat. Add garlic and cook for 1-2 minutes until fragrant.
2. Add shrimp and cook until pink and opaque, about 3-4 minutes.
3. Pour in the coconut milk, lemon juice, salt, pepper, and red pepper flakes. Bring to a simmer and cook for another 5 minutes.
4. Adjust seasoning as needed and garnish with fresh parsley. Serve over pasta or rice.

Coconut Milk Pancakes

Ingredients:

- 1 1/2 cups all-purpose flour
- 1 tbsp sugar
- 1 tbsp baking powder
- 1/2 tsp salt
- 1 1/4 cups coconut milk
- 1 egg
- 2 tbsp melted coconut oil or butter
- 1 tsp vanilla extract

Instructions:

1. In a large bowl, whisk together flour, sugar, baking powder, and salt.
2. In another bowl, combine coconut milk, egg, melted coconut oil, and vanilla extract.
3. Pour the wet ingredients into the dry ingredients and stir until just combined (lumps are okay).
4. Heat a griddle or non-stick pan over medium heat and lightly grease with coconut oil or butter.
5. Pour batter onto the griddle in small rounds and cook until bubbles form on the surface. Flip and cook until golden brown on both sides.
6. Serve warm with maple syrup or your favorite toppings.

Creamy Coconut Milk Mashed Potatoes

Ingredients:

- 2 lbs potatoes, peeled and cubed
- 1 can (14 oz) coconut milk
- 2 tbsp olive oil or butter
- Salt and pepper to taste
- Fresh chives for garnish (optional)

Instructions:

1. Boil potatoes in a large pot of salted water until tender, about 15-20 minutes. Drain and return to the pot.
2. In a small saucepan, heat coconut milk and olive oil (or butter) until warm.
3. Mash the potatoes, then stir in the warm coconut milk mixture. Season with salt and pepper.
4. Garnish with fresh chives and serve.

Coconut Milk Chia Pudding

Ingredients:

- 1 can (14 oz) coconut milk
- 1/4 cup chia seeds
- 2 tbsp maple syrup or honey
- 1/2 tsp vanilla extract
- Fresh fruit for topping (optional)

Instructions:

1. In a bowl, whisk together coconut milk, chia seeds, maple syrup, and vanilla extract.
2. Cover and refrigerate for at least 4 hours or overnight, allowing the chia seeds to absorb the liquid and thicken.
3. Stir before serving and top with fresh fruit if desired.

Coconut Milk Tofu Stir-Fry

Ingredients:

- 1 block firm tofu, cubed
- 1 can (14 oz) coconut milk
- 2 tbsp soy sauce
- 1 tbsp sesame oil
- 1 red bell pepper, sliced
- 1 cup broccoli florets
- 1/2 cup sliced carrots
- 2 garlic cloves, minced
- 1 tbsp grated ginger
- 2 tbsp green onions, chopped for garnish

Instructions:

1. In a large pan, heat sesame oil over medium heat. Add tofu cubes and cook until golden brown on all sides, about 5-7 minutes. Remove from the pan and set aside.
2. In the same pan, add garlic, ginger, bell pepper, broccoli, and carrots. Sauté for 5-7 minutes, until the vegetables are tender.
3. Stir in coconut milk and soy sauce, then return tofu to the pan. Simmer for 5-10 minutes, until heated through and the sauce thickens.
4. Garnish with green onions and serve hot over rice or noodles.

Coconut Curry Lentils

Ingredients:

- 1 cup dried lentils, rinsed
- 1 can (14 oz) coconut milk
- 2 cups vegetable broth
- 1 onion, diced
- 2 garlic cloves, minced
- 1 tbsp grated ginger
- 1 tbsp curry powder
- 1 tsp turmeric
- 1/2 tsp cumin
- 1/2 tsp paprika
- Salt and pepper to taste
- 1 tbsp olive oil
- Fresh cilantro for garnish

Instructions:

1. Heat olive oil in a large pot over medium heat. Add diced onion and sauté for 5-6 minutes until softened.
2. Add garlic and ginger, cooking for an additional minute.
3. Stir in curry powder, turmeric, cumin, paprika, salt, and pepper. Cook for 1-2 minutes to release the flavors.
4. Add lentils, coconut milk, and vegetable broth. Bring to a boil, then reduce heat and simmer, covered, for 25-30 minutes or until lentils are tender.
5. Adjust seasoning if necessary. Garnish with fresh cilantro and serve.

Coconut Milk Ice Cream

Ingredients:

- 2 cans (14 oz each) coconut milk
- 1/2 cup sugar or sweetener of choice
- 1 tsp vanilla extract
- Pinch of salt

Instructions:

1. In a mixing bowl, whisk together coconut milk, sugar, vanilla extract, and a pinch of salt until the sugar dissolves.
2. Pour the mixture into an ice cream maker and churn according to the manufacturer's instructions, typically for 20-25 minutes.
3. Transfer the churned ice cream to a container and freeze for at least 4 hours before serving.

Coconut Milk Chicken Soup

Ingredients:

- 1 lb chicken breast, cooked and shredded
- 1 can (14 oz) coconut milk
- 4 cups chicken broth
- 2 carrots, diced
- 2 celery stalks, diced
- 1 onion, diced
- 2 garlic cloves, minced
- 1 tsp turmeric
- 1/2 tsp ground ginger
- Salt and pepper to taste
- Fresh cilantro for garnish

Instructions:

1. In a large pot, sauté the onion, garlic, carrots, and celery until soft, about 5 minutes.
2. Add turmeric, ground ginger, salt, and pepper, and cook for 1 minute.
3. Pour in the coconut milk and chicken broth. Bring to a simmer and cook for 15 minutes.
4. Add the shredded chicken and cook for another 10 minutes until heated through.
5. Garnish with fresh cilantro and serve warm.

Vegan Coconut Milk Chocolate Mousse

Ingredients:

- 1 can (14 oz) coconut milk (full-fat)
- 8 oz dark chocolate (70% cocoa or more)
- 2 tbsp maple syrup or sweetener of choice
- 1 tsp vanilla extract
- Pinch of salt

Instructions:

1. In a small saucepan, gently heat the coconut milk until it starts to simmer.
2. Break the dark chocolate into pieces and stir it into the coconut milk until melted and smooth.
3. Remove from heat and stir in maple syrup, vanilla extract, and a pinch of salt.
4. Let the mixture cool for a few minutes before refrigerating for 1-2 hours until set.
5. Serve chilled, optionally garnished with berries or coconut flakes.

Coconut Milk Smoothie Bowl

Ingredients:

- 1 frozen banana
- 1/2 cup coconut milk
- 1/2 cup frozen berries (strawberries, blueberries, or mixed)
- 1 tbsp chia seeds or flaxseeds
- Toppings: granola, coconut flakes, sliced fruit, nuts, seeds

Instructions:

1. In a blender, combine the frozen banana, coconut milk, frozen berries, and chia seeds. Blend until smooth and creamy.
2. Pour into a bowl and top with your favorite toppings like granola, coconut flakes, fresh fruit, and nuts.
3. Serve immediately as a healthy breakfast or snack.

Coconut Milk Rice Pilaf

Ingredients:

- 1 cup jasmine rice
- 1 can (14 oz) coconut milk
- 1 cup water
- 1/2 onion, diced
- 2 garlic cloves, minced
- 1/2 tsp cumin
- Salt to taste
- Fresh cilantro for garnish

Instructions:

1. In a large pan, sauté diced onion and garlic in a little oil over medium heat until softened, about 5 minutes.
2. Stir in the rice and cumin, cooking for 1-2 minutes until the rice is lightly toasted.
3. Add coconut milk, water, and salt, and bring to a boil.
4. Reduce heat, cover, and simmer for 15-20 minutes, or until the rice is tender and the liquid is absorbed.
5. Garnish with fresh cilantro and serve.

Spicy Coconut Milk Noodles

Ingredients:

- 8 oz rice noodles
- 1 can (14 oz) coconut milk
- 2 tbsp soy sauce
- 1 tbsp sriracha or chili paste
- 1 tbsp lime juice
- 1 tbsp brown sugar
- 2 garlic cloves, minced
- 1 tsp grated ginger
- 1/4 cup chopped peanuts (optional)
- Fresh cilantro for garnish

Instructions:

1. Cook rice noodles according to package instructions. Drain and set aside.
2. In a pan, heat coconut milk, soy sauce, sriracha, lime juice, and brown sugar. Stir to combine and bring to a simmer.
3. Add garlic and ginger and cook for 2-3 minutes.
4. Toss the cooked noodles in the coconut sauce, stirring to coat evenly.
5. Garnish with chopped peanuts and fresh cilantro before serving.

Coconut Milk Braised Beef

Ingredients:

- 1.5 lbs beef stew meat, cubed
- 1 can (14 oz) coconut milk
- 1 onion, sliced
- 3 garlic cloves, minced
- 2 tbsp soy sauce
- 1 tbsp brown sugar
- 1 tsp ground cumin
- 1 tsp ground coriander
- 2 cups beef broth
- Salt and pepper to taste
- Fresh parsley for garnish

Instructions:

1. In a large pot, brown the beef cubes in a little oil over medium heat. Remove and set aside.
2. In the same pot, sauté onion and garlic until softened, about 5 minutes.
3. Add cumin, coriander, soy sauce, and brown sugar. Stir to combine.
4. Return the beef to the pot, then pour in coconut milk and beef broth. Bring to a simmer.
5. Cover and cook on low for 2-3 hours, until the beef is tender and the flavors meld.
6. Adjust seasoning with salt and pepper, garnish with parsley, and serve.

Coconut Milk Tapioca Pudding

Ingredients:

- 1/2 cup small tapioca pearls
- 1 can (14 oz) coconut milk
- 2 cups water
- 1/4 cup sugar
- 1 tsp vanilla extract
- Pinch of salt

Instructions:

1. In a medium saucepan, combine tapioca pearls, coconut milk, and water. Bring to a simmer over medium heat.
2. Stir occasionally and cook for 20-25 minutes, or until the tapioca pearls become translucent and the pudding thickens.
3. Add sugar, vanilla extract, and a pinch of salt. Stir well and cook for another 5 minutes.
4. Remove from heat and let it cool for 10-15 minutes before serving. Serve warm or chilled.

Coconut Milk Mango Lassi

Ingredients:

- 1 cup coconut milk
- 1 ripe mango, peeled and diced
- 1/2 cup plain yogurt or coconut yogurt (for a vegan option)
- 1 tbsp honey or maple syrup
- 1/2 tsp ground cardamom
- Ice cubes (optional)

Instructions:

1. Place the coconut milk, mango, yogurt, honey, and cardamom into a blender.
2. Blend until smooth and creamy. If desired, add a few ice cubes to chill.
3. Taste and adjust sweetness with more honey or syrup if needed.
4. Pour into glasses and serve chilled.

Coconut and Lime Shrimp

Ingredients:

- 1 lb shrimp, peeled and deveined
- 1 can (14 oz) coconut milk
- 2 tbsp fresh lime juice
- 2 garlic cloves, minced
- 1 tbsp grated ginger
- 1 tbsp olive oil
- Salt and pepper to taste
- Fresh cilantro for garnish

Instructions:

1. Heat olive oil in a large pan over medium heat. Add garlic and ginger, cooking for 1-2 minutes until fragrant.
2. Add shrimp to the pan and cook for 2-3 minutes per side until pink and cooked through.
3. Pour in the coconut milk and lime juice. Stir to combine, season with salt and pepper, and simmer for 5 minutes.
4. Garnish with fresh cilantro and serve with rice or vegetables.

Coconut Milk Panna Cotta

Ingredients:

- 2 cans (14 oz each) coconut milk
- 1/2 cup sugar
- 1 tsp vanilla extract
- 2 1/2 tsp agar agar powder (for a vegan option) or gelatin (for non-vegan option)
- Fresh berries for topping

Instructions:

1. In a saucepan, heat the coconut milk and sugar over medium heat, stirring until the sugar dissolves.
2. Sprinkle the agar agar or gelatin into the mixture and stir well. Bring to a simmer and cook for 2-3 minutes, allowing the mixture to thicken slightly.
3. Remove from heat and stir in vanilla extract.
4. Pour the mixture into molds or glasses and refrigerate for 4-6 hours or until set.
5. Serve with fresh berries on top.

Coconut Milk and Almond Cake

Ingredients:

- 1 1/2 cups almond flour
- 1/2 cup coconut milk
- 3 eggs
- 1/4 cup maple syrup or honey
- 1 tsp vanilla extract
- 1/2 tsp baking powder
- Pinch of salt
- Sliced almonds for topping (optional)

Instructions:

1. Preheat the oven to 350°F (175°C) and grease a cake pan.
2. In a bowl, whisk together almond flour, baking powder, and salt.
3. In another bowl, beat the eggs, then add coconut milk, maple syrup, and vanilla extract. Mix until smooth.
4. Combine the wet and dry ingredients and stir until well incorporated.
5. Pour the batter into the prepared cake pan and bake for 25-30 minutes or until a toothpick inserted comes out clean.
6. Let the cake cool, then top with sliced almonds if desired before serving.

Coconut Milk Quinoa Salad

Ingredients:

- 1 cup cooked quinoa
- 1/2 cup coconut milk
- 1/2 cup chopped cucumber
- 1/2 cup chopped bell pepper
- 1/4 cup chopped red onion
- 1 tbsp olive oil
- 2 tbsp fresh lime juice
- 1 tbsp chopped cilantro
- Salt and pepper to taste

Instructions:

1. In a large bowl, combine cooked quinoa with cucumber, bell pepper, and red onion.
2. In a separate small bowl, whisk together coconut milk, olive oil, lime juice, cilantro, salt, and pepper.
3. Pour the dressing over the quinoa salad and toss to combine.
4. Chill the salad in the refrigerator for 30 minutes before serving.

Coconut Milk Popsicles

Ingredients:

- 1 can (14 oz) coconut milk
- 1/4 cup honey or maple syrup
- 1 cup fresh fruit (mango, berries, or kiwi)
- 1 tsp vanilla extract

Instructions:

1. Blend the coconut milk, honey, and vanilla extract until smooth.
2. Add your choice of fresh fruit to the mixture or layer it into the popsicle molds.
3. Pour the coconut milk mixture over the fruit in the molds.
4. Insert sticks and freeze for 4-6 hours until fully frozen.
5. To release, run warm water over the outside of the molds for a few seconds before removing the popsicles.

Coconut Milk Rice with Turmeric

Ingredients:

- 1 cup jasmine rice
- 1 can (14 oz) coconut milk
- 1 cup water
- 1 tsp turmeric
- 1/2 tsp cumin
- Salt to taste

Instructions:

1. Rinse the rice under cold water until the water runs clear.
2. In a pot, combine rice, coconut milk, water, turmeric, cumin, and salt.
3. Bring to a boil, then reduce heat to low, cover, and simmer for 15-20 minutes until the rice is tender and the liquid is absorbed.
4. Fluff the rice with a fork and serve.

Coconut Milk Roasted Squash Soup

Ingredients:

- 1 medium butternut squash, peeled, cubed
- 1 onion, chopped
- 2 garlic cloves, minced
- 1 can (14 oz) coconut milk
- 3 cups vegetable broth
- 1 tsp ground cinnamon
- 1/2 tsp ground nutmeg
- Salt and pepper to taste
- Olive oil for roasting

Instructions:

1. Preheat the oven to 400°F (200°C). Toss cubed squash with olive oil, salt, and pepper, then roast for 25-30 minutes, until tender.
2. In a large pot, sauté onion and garlic until softened, about 5 minutes.
3. Add roasted squash, coconut milk, vegetable broth, cinnamon, and nutmeg. Bring to a simmer and cook for 10 minutes.
4. Use an immersion blender or transfer the soup to a blender to puree until smooth.
5. Adjust seasoning with salt and pepper, then serve warm.

Coconut Milk & Chia Breakfast Porridge

Ingredients:

- 1/2 cup chia seeds
- 1 can (14 oz) coconut milk
- 1 tbsp maple syrup or honey
- 1/2 tsp vanilla extract
- Fresh fruit and nuts for topping

Instructions:

1. In a bowl, mix chia seeds, coconut milk, maple syrup, and vanilla extract.
2. Stir well, cover, and refrigerate overnight or for at least 6 hours to allow the chia seeds to absorb the liquid and thicken.
3. In the morning, stir the porridge, top with fresh fruit and nuts, and serve.

Coconut Milk Vegan Mac and Cheese

Ingredients:

- 1 cup elbow macaroni (or pasta of choice)
- 1 can (14 oz) coconut milk
- 1/4 cup nutritional yeast
- 2 tbsp olive oil
- 1 tbsp Dijon mustard
- 1 tsp garlic powder
- 1/2 tsp turmeric
- Salt and pepper to taste
- 1/2 cup steamed cauliflower (optional, for added creaminess)

Instructions:

1. Cook the pasta according to package instructions, then drain and set aside.
2. In a saucepan, combine coconut milk, nutritional yeast, olive oil, Dijon mustard, garlic powder, turmeric, salt, and pepper. Stir until smooth and bring to a simmer.
3. Add steamed cauliflower (if using) and blend until smooth for a creamier texture.
4. Toss the cooked pasta with the sauce and serve immediately.

Coconut Milk and Lemon Curd Tart

Ingredients:

- 1 pre-baked tart crust (store-bought or homemade)
- 1 can (14 oz) coconut milk
- 1/2 cup lemon juice (about 2-3 lemons)
- 1/4 cup sugar or maple syrup
- 3 tbsp cornstarch or arrowroot powder
- 1/4 tsp turmeric (for color, optional)
- Zest of 1 lemon
- 1/2 tsp vanilla extract

Instructions:

1. In a saucepan, combine coconut milk, lemon juice, sugar, cornstarch, turmeric (if using), and lemon zest. Whisk until smooth.
2. Bring the mixture to a simmer over medium heat, stirring constantly, until thickened (about 5 minutes).
3. Remove from heat and stir in vanilla extract.
4. Pour the lemon curd into the pre-baked tart crust and smooth out the top.
5. Chill in the refrigerator for at least 2 hours before serving.

Spicy Coconut Milk Fish Curry

Ingredients:

- 1 lb white fish fillets (such as cod or tilapia), cut into chunks
- 1 can (14 oz) coconut milk
- 1 onion, chopped
- 2 garlic cloves, minced
- 1-inch piece ginger, grated
- 1 tbsp curry powder
- 1 tsp chili powder (or to taste)
- 1/2 tsp turmeric
- 1 tbsp fish sauce (optional)
- 1 tbsp lime juice
- Fresh cilantro for garnish
- Olive oil for sautéing

Instructions:

1. Heat olive oil in a large pan over medium heat. Sauté the onion, garlic, and ginger until fragrant and softened (about 5 minutes).
2. Stir in curry powder, chili powder, and turmeric. Cook for 1 minute to toast the spices.
3. Add coconut milk and bring to a simmer. Cook for 5 minutes to thicken the sauce.
4. Add the fish chunks and cook for 5-7 minutes, until the fish is cooked through.
5. Stir in fish sauce and lime juice, then garnish with fresh cilantro.
6. Serve with rice or naan bread.

Coconut Milk and Banana Smoothie

Ingredients:

- 1 ripe banana
- 1 cup coconut milk
- 1/2 cup ice cubes
- 1 tbsp honey or maple syrup
- 1/4 tsp cinnamon (optional)

Instructions:

1. Place the banana, coconut milk, ice cubes, honey, and cinnamon (if using) in a blender.
2. Blend until smooth and creamy.
3. Taste and adjust sweetness as desired.
4. Pour into glasses and serve chilled.

Coconut Milk Porridge with Fruit

Ingredients:

- 1/2 cup rolled oats
- 1 can (14 oz) coconut milk
- 1 cup water
- 1 tbsp maple syrup or honey
- 1/2 tsp cinnamon
- Fresh fruit (berries, banana, mango) for topping
- Chopped nuts or seeds for topping (optional)

Instructions:

1. In a saucepan, combine oats, coconut milk, water, maple syrup, and cinnamon.
2. Bring to a boil, then reduce heat and simmer for 5-7 minutes, stirring occasionally, until the oats are tender and the porridge has thickened.
3. Serve topped with fresh fruit and chopped nuts or seeds.

Coconut Milk Chicken and Sweet Potato Stew

Ingredients:

- 2 chicken breasts or thighs, diced
- 2 medium sweet potatoes, peeled and cubed
- 1 can (14 oz) coconut milk
- 2 cups chicken broth
- 1 onion, chopped
- 2 garlic cloves, minced
- 1 tbsp curry powder
- 1 tsp cumin
- 1 tsp paprika
- Salt and pepper to taste
- Fresh cilantro for garnish

Instructions:

1. In a large pot, heat olive oil over medium heat. Add the chicken and cook until browned. Remove and set aside.
2. In the same pot, sauté the onion and garlic until softened (about 5 minutes).
3. Stir in curry powder, cumin, paprika, salt, and pepper. Cook for 1 minute to release the spices' aromas.
4. Add sweet potatoes, coconut milk, chicken broth, and the cooked chicken back into the pot. Bring to a boil.
5. Reduce heat and simmer for 20-25 minutes until the sweet potatoes are tender and the stew has thickened.
6. Garnish with fresh cilantro before serving.

Coconut Milk Gravy for Biscuits

Ingredients:

- 1 can (14 oz) coconut milk
- 2 tbsp flour (or gluten-free flour)
- 1 tbsp olive oil
- 1/2 tsp garlic powder
- Salt and pepper to taste
- 1/2 tsp fresh thyme (optional)

Instructions:

1. In a saucepan, heat olive oil over medium heat. Whisk in the flour and cook for 1-2 minutes to form a roux.
2. Gradually whisk in coconut milk, garlic powder, salt, and pepper. Cook, stirring constantly, until the gravy thickens (about 5 minutes).
3. Stir in fresh thyme, if using, and adjust seasoning with salt and pepper.
4. Serve hot over biscuits.

Coconut Milk and Pineapple Chutney

Ingredients:

- 1 cup diced pineapple
- 1/2 cup coconut milk
- 1/4 cup apple cider vinegar
- 2 tbsp brown sugar
- 1 small onion, chopped
- 1 tbsp grated ginger
- 1/4 tsp ground cloves
- 1/4 tsp ground cinnamon
- Pinch of salt

Instructions:

1. In a saucepan, combine pineapple, coconut milk, apple cider vinegar, brown sugar, onion, ginger, cloves, cinnamon, and salt.
2. Bring to a simmer over medium heat, then cook for 15-20 minutes, stirring occasionally, until the chutney thickens.
3. Let cool and refrigerate for up to a week. Serve with grilled meats, rice, or as a topping for sandwiches.

Coconut Milk Cauliflower Soup

Ingredients:

- 1 large head of cauliflower, chopped into florets
- 1 can (14 oz) coconut milk
- 4 cups vegetable broth
- 1 onion, chopped
- 2 garlic cloves, minced
- 1 tbsp olive oil
- 1/2 tsp turmeric
- Salt and pepper to taste
- Fresh parsley or cilantro for garnish

Instructions:

1. Heat olive oil in a large pot over medium heat. Sauté the onion and garlic until softened, about 5 minutes.
2. Add cauliflower, turmeric, salt, and pepper. Stir to coat the cauliflower in the spices.
3. Pour in vegetable broth and bring to a boil. Reduce the heat and simmer for 15-20 minutes, or until the cauliflower is tender.
4. Stir in coconut milk and cook for an additional 5 minutes.
5. Use an immersion blender to puree the soup until smooth (or blend in batches in a regular blender).
6. Serve hot, garnished with fresh parsley or cilantro.

Coconut Milk Scones with Jam

Ingredients:

- 2 cups all-purpose flour
- 1/4 cup coconut sugar or regular sugar
- 1 tbsp baking powder
- 1/2 tsp salt
- 1/2 cup coconut milk
- 1/4 cup coconut oil, melted
- 1 tsp vanilla extract
- Jam of your choice for serving

Instructions:

1. Preheat your oven to 400°F (200°C) and line a baking sheet with parchment paper.
2. In a large bowl, whisk together flour, sugar, baking powder, and salt.
3. In a separate bowl, combine coconut milk, melted coconut oil, and vanilla extract.
4. Pour the wet ingredients into the dry ingredients and stir until just combined.
5. Turn the dough out onto a floured surface and knead gently a few times. Pat the dough into a 1-inch thick circle, then cut into 8 wedges.
6. Place the scones on the prepared baking sheet and bake for 12-15 minutes, until golden brown.
7. Serve warm with jam.

Coconut Milk Vegetable Stew

Ingredients:

- 2 cups coconut milk
- 1 can (14 oz) diced tomatoes
- 2 cups vegetable broth
- 1 onion, chopped
- 2 garlic cloves, minced
- 2 carrots, peeled and diced
- 2 potatoes, peeled and diced
- 1 zucchini, chopped
- 1 cup green beans, chopped
- 1/2 tsp cumin
- 1/2 tsp paprika
- Salt and pepper to taste
- Fresh basil or parsley for garnish

Instructions:

1. Heat olive oil in a large pot over medium heat. Sauté onion and garlic until softened, about 5 minutes.
2. Add carrots, potatoes, zucchini, and green beans. Stir to combine.
3. Pour in coconut milk, diced tomatoes, and vegetable broth. Stir in cumin, paprika, salt, and pepper.
4. Bring to a boil, then reduce heat and simmer for 20-25 minutes, until the vegetables are tender.
5. Garnish with fresh basil or parsley before serving.

Thai Coconut Milk Curry

Ingredients:

- 1 can (14 oz) coconut milk
- 2 tbsp red curry paste
- 1 lb chicken, tofu, or shrimp (optional)
- 1 onion, chopped
- 1 bell pepper, sliced
- 1 carrot, thinly sliced
- 1/2 cup mushrooms, sliced
- 1 tbsp soy sauce or tamari
- 1 tbsp lime juice
- 1/2 tsp sugar
- Fresh cilantro for garnish
- Rice for serving

Instructions:

1. Heat a large pan over medium heat and sauté onion until softened, about 5 minutes.
2. Stir in red curry paste and cook for 1 minute, then add coconut milk, soy sauce, lime juice, and sugar.
3. Add your choice of protein (chicken, tofu, or shrimp) and simmer for 10-15 minutes, until cooked through.
4. Add the bell pepper, carrot, and mushrooms, and cook for an additional 5 minutes until the vegetables are tender.
5. Serve over rice and garnish with fresh cilantro.

Coconut Milk Brown Rice Pudding

Ingredients:

- 1 cup cooked brown rice
- 1 can (14 oz) coconut milk
- 1/4 cup maple syrup or sugar
- 1 tsp vanilla extract
- 1/4 tsp cinnamon
- Pinch of salt
- Fresh berries or chopped nuts for garnish

Instructions:

1. In a saucepan, combine cooked brown rice, coconut milk, maple syrup, vanilla extract, cinnamon, and salt.
2. Bring to a simmer over medium heat and cook for 10-15 minutes, stirring occasionally, until the mixture thickens to a pudding-like consistency.
3. Remove from heat and let cool slightly.
4. Serve warm or chilled, topped with fresh berries or chopped nuts.

Coconut Milk Green Smoothie

Ingredients:

- 1 cup coconut milk
- 1 banana
- 1 cup spinach or kale
- 1/2 cup frozen mango or pineapple
- 1 tbsp chia seeds or flaxseeds
- 1/2 tsp spirulina (optional)
- Ice cubes (optional)

Instructions:

1. Place all ingredients into a blender.
2. Blend until smooth, adding ice cubes for a thicker consistency if desired.
3. Taste and adjust sweetness or thickness by adding more coconut milk or fruit.
4. Serve immediately.

Coconut Milk Ice Cream Bars

Ingredients:

- 1 can (14 oz) coconut milk
- 1/4 cup maple syrup or honey
- 1 tsp vanilla extract
- 1 cup dark chocolate, melted
- 1/4 cup shredded coconut (optional)

Instructions:

1. In a bowl, combine coconut milk, maple syrup, and vanilla extract.
2. Pour the mixture into ice cream bar molds and freeze for at least 3-4 hours, or until firm.
3. Once frozen, dip the bars into the melted chocolate, then sprinkle with shredded coconut if desired.
4. Freeze again for 30 minutes to set the chocolate, then serve.

Coconut Milk Caramel Sauce

Ingredients:

- 1 can (14 oz) coconut milk
- 1/2 cup brown sugar
- 1/4 cup maple syrup
- 1/2 tsp vanilla extract
- Pinch of salt

Instructions:

1. In a saucepan, combine coconut milk, brown sugar, and maple syrup.
2. Bring to a boil, then reduce the heat and simmer for 10-15 minutes, stirring occasionally, until the sauce thickens.
3. Stir in vanilla extract and salt, then remove from heat.
4. Let the caramel sauce cool slightly before serving. It will continue to thicken as it cools.

Coconut Milk Granola Bars

Ingredients:

- 1 cup rolled oats
- 1/2 cup shredded coconut
- 1/4 cup coconut milk
- 1/4 cup honey or maple syrup
- 1/2 tsp vanilla extract
- 1/4 cup nuts or seeds (optional)
- 1/4 cup dried fruit (optional)

Instructions:

1. Preheat your oven to 350°F (175°C) and line a baking dish with parchment paper.
2. In a bowl, combine oats, shredded coconut, and any optional nuts or seeds.
3. In a small saucepan, warm coconut milk, honey, and vanilla extract over medium heat until combined.
4. Pour the wet ingredients over the dry ingredients and stir until well mixed.
5. Press the mixture firmly into the prepared baking dish and bake for 15-20 minutes, until golden brown.
6. Let cool completely before cutting into bars.

Coconut Milk Banana Bread

Ingredients:

- 1 cup mashed ripe bananas (about 2-3 bananas)
- 1 can (14 oz) coconut milk
- 1/2 cup coconut oil, melted
- 1/2 cup brown sugar or maple syrup
- 2 cups all-purpose flour
- 1 tsp baking powder
- 1/2 tsp baking soda
- 1/4 tsp salt
- 1 tsp vanilla extract
- 1/2 tsp cinnamon (optional)
- 1/2 cup chopped walnuts or chocolate chips (optional)

Instructions:

1. Preheat your oven to 350°F (175°C) and grease a loaf pan.
2. In a large bowl, mix together the mashed bananas, coconut milk, melted coconut oil, and vanilla extract.
3. In a separate bowl, whisk together the flour, baking powder, baking soda, salt, and cinnamon (if using).
4. Slowly add the dry ingredients into the wet ingredients and mix until just combined.
5. Fold in the walnuts or chocolate chips if desired.
6. Pour the batter into the prepared loaf pan and smooth the top.
7. Bake for 50-60 minutes, or until a toothpick inserted into the center comes out clean.
8. Let the bread cool in the pan for 10 minutes before transferring it to a wire rack to cool completely.

Coconut Milk Pumpkin Soup

Ingredients:

- 1 can (15 oz) pumpkin puree
- 1 can (14 oz) coconut milk
- 1 onion, chopped
- 2 garlic cloves, minced
- 2 cups vegetable broth
- 1/2 tsp cinnamon
- 1/4 tsp nutmeg
- 1/4 tsp ground ginger
- Salt and pepper to taste
- 1 tbsp olive oil
- Fresh parsley or coconut cream for garnish (optional)

Instructions:

1. Heat olive oil in a large pot over medium heat. Add onion and garlic, sautéing until softened, about 5 minutes.
2. Add pumpkin puree, coconut milk, vegetable broth, cinnamon, nutmeg, ginger, salt, and pepper. Stir to combine.
3. Bring the soup to a simmer, then reduce the heat and cook for 15-20 minutes, allowing the flavors to meld.
4. Use an immersion blender to blend the soup until smooth, or transfer to a blender in batches.
5. Garnish with fresh parsley or a swirl of coconut cream if desired.
6. Serve hot with crusty bread or crackers.

Coconut Milk Rice Cake

Ingredients:

- 2 cups cooked jasmine rice
- 1/2 can (7 oz) coconut milk
- 1/4 cup sugar (or more to taste)
- 1/4 tsp salt
- 1/4 cup shredded coconut (optional)
- 1 tsp vanilla extract
- Fruit toppings like mango, berries, or bananas (optional)

Instructions:

1. In a saucepan, combine coconut milk, sugar, and salt. Bring to a simmer over medium heat, stirring until the sugar dissolves.
2. Stir in the cooked rice, mixing well to coat the rice with the coconut milk mixture.
3. Continue cooking for 5-7 minutes, until the rice absorbs the liquid and becomes creamy.
4. Stir in vanilla extract and shredded coconut if using.
5. Transfer the mixture into a greased baking dish and press it down evenly.
6. Allow to cool to room temperature, then refrigerate for at least 2 hours before slicing into squares or bars.
7. Top with fresh fruit or a drizzle of extra coconut milk if desired.

Coconut Milk Spiced Pudding

Ingredients:

- 1 can (14 oz) coconut milk
- 1/4 cup sugar or maple syrup
- 1/4 tsp cinnamon
- 1/4 tsp nutmeg
- 1/4 tsp ground ginger
- 1 tbsp cornstarch
- 1/2 tsp vanilla extract

Instructions:

1. In a medium saucepan, combine coconut milk, sugar, cinnamon, nutmeg, and ginger. Bring to a simmer over medium heat, stirring occasionally.
2. In a small bowl, dissolve cornstarch in 2 tbsp of cold coconut milk, then whisk this mixture into the saucepan.
3. Continue stirring the mixture until it thickens, about 5-7 minutes.
4. Remove from heat and stir in vanilla extract.
5. Pour the pudding into individual serving bowls and let it cool to room temperature.
6. Refrigerate for at least 1 hour before serving, garnished with cinnamon or shredded coconut if desired.

Coconut Milk Smoothie with Berries

Ingredients:

- 1 cup coconut milk
- 1/2 cup mixed frozen berries (strawberries, blueberries, raspberries)
- 1 ripe banana
- 1 tbsp honey or maple syrup (optional)
- Ice cubes (optional)

Instructions:

1. In a blender, combine coconut milk, frozen berries, banana, and honey or maple syrup if using.
2. Blend until smooth, adding ice cubes if you prefer a thicker consistency.
3. Taste and adjust sweetness by adding more honey or syrup if needed.
4. Serve immediately in a chilled glass.

Coconut Milk Chicken Tikka Masala

Ingredients:

- 1 lb chicken breast, cubed
- 1 can (14 oz) coconut milk
- 2 tbsp tikka masala paste
- 1 onion, chopped
- 2 garlic cloves, minced
- 1 tsp grated ginger
- 1 tbsp vegetable oil
- 1/2 tsp turmeric
- 1/2 tsp cumin
- 1/2 tsp garam masala
- 1/2 tsp paprika
- Salt and pepper to taste
- Fresh cilantro for garnish
- Cooked rice for serving

Instructions:

1. In a large skillet, heat vegetable oil over medium heat. Add onion and cook until softened, about 5 minutes.
2. Add garlic, ginger, turmeric, cumin, garam masala, paprika, salt, and pepper. Cook for 1-2 minutes until fragrant.
3. Stir in the chicken cubes and cook until browned on all sides, about 5-7 minutes.
4. Add tikka masala paste and coconut milk, stirring to combine.
5. Bring the mixture to a simmer, then reduce the heat and cook for an additional 15-20 minutes, until the chicken is cooked through and the sauce thickens.
6. Serve the chicken tikka masala over cooked rice and garnish with fresh cilantro.

www.ingramcontent.com/pod-product-compliance
Lightning Source LLC
LaVergne TN
LVHW081334060526
838201LV00055B/2636